EARTH'S
HISTORY
THROUGH
ROCKS

THE HIGHEST PEAK

HOW
MOUNT EVEREST
FORMED

JENNA TOLLI

PowerKiDS
press
New York

Published in 2020 by The Rosen Publishing Group, Inc.
29 East 21st Street, New York, NY 10010

First Edition

Editor: Sarah Machajewski
Book Design: Tanya Dellaccio

Photo Credits: Cover Education Images/Universal Images Group/Getty Images; p. 5 THEPALMER/ DigitalVision Vectors/Getty Images; p. 5 Keystone/Hulton Archive/Getty Images; p. 6 Time & Life Pictures/ The LIFE Picture Collection/Getty Images; p. 7 Science & Society Picture Library/SSPL/Getty Images; p. 8 https://upload.wikimedia.org/wikipedia/commons/6/65/Alfred_Wegener_ca.1924-30.jpg; p. 9 bortonia/DigitalVision Vectors/Getty Images; p. 11 (top) FrankRamspott/DigitalVision Vectors/ Getty Images; p. 11 (bottom) Designua/Shutterstock.com; p. 13 (bottom) Dan Shugar/Aurora/Getty Images; pp. 13 (top), 29 Vixit/Shutterstock.com; p. 15 Olga Danylenko/Shutterstock.com; p. 17 (top) Taylor Weidman/LightRocket/Getty Images; p. 17 Boris Rezvantsev/Shutterstock.com; p. 19 ET1972/ Shutterstock.com; p. 21 (top) Westend61/Getty Images; p. 21 (bottom) Nigel Killeen/Moment/Getty Images; p. 23 Godong/Universal Images Group/Getty Images; p. 25 (top) Alex Treadway/National Geographic/Getty Images; p. 25 (bottom) Jason Maehl/Moment/Getty Images; p. 27 maps4media/Getty Images News/Getty Images; p. 30 Daniel Prudek/Shutterstock.com.

Library of Congress Cataloging-in-Publication Data

Names: Tolli, Jenna, author.
Title: The highest peak : how Mount Everest formed / Jenna Tolli.
Other titles: How Mount Everest formed
Description: New York : PowerKids Press, [2020] | Series: Earth's history
  through rocks | Includes index.
Identifiers: LCCN 2018049464| ISBN 9781725301443 (pbk.) | ISBN 9781725301467
  (library bound) | ISBN 9781725301450 (6 pack)
Subjects: LCSH: Everest, Mount (China and Nepal)–Juvenile literature. |
  Geology–Everest, Mount (China and Nepal)–Juvenile literature.
Classification: LCC DS495.8.E9 T65 2020 | DDC 555.496–dc23
LC record available at https://lccn.loc.gov/2018049464

Manufactured in the United States of America

CPSIA Compliance Information: Batch #CSPK19. For Further Information contact Rosen Publishing, New York, New York at 1-800-237-9932.

CONTENTS

THE HIGHEST PEAK ON EARTH

Where is the highest peak in the world? It's at the top of Mount Everest! This huge mountain is part of the Himalayas, a mountain range that spreads across six countries in Asia and is about 1,500 miles (2,414 km) long. There are over 110 mountain peaks in this range. Mount Everest, located on the border of Tibet and Nepal, is the highest peak.

The weather on Mount Everest is extremely cold. Even in the warmest months, the temperature is still below freezing at a bitter -2° Fahrenheit (-19° Celsius). Wind speeds at the **summit** are very fast, too. They average around 100 miles (161 km) per hour, but the highest winds have been recorded at 175 miles (281.6 km) per hour.

DIFFERENT MEASUREMENTS

Scientists disagree on the exact height of Mount Everest. The snow level at the peak changes, and different methods of measuring can provide different results. Scientists have also questioned whether recent destructive earthquakes in Nepal have changed the height of the mountain. At this time, Nepal and China agree that the current height is around 29,029 feet (8,848 m).

TENZING
NORGAY

SIR
EDMUND
HILLARY

READING THE ROCKS

SIR EDMUND HILLARY AND TENZING NORGAY WERE THE FIRST EXPLORERS TO REACH THE SUMMIT OF MOUNT EVEREST. THEY CLIMBED TO THE TOP TOGETHER ON MAY 29, 1953.

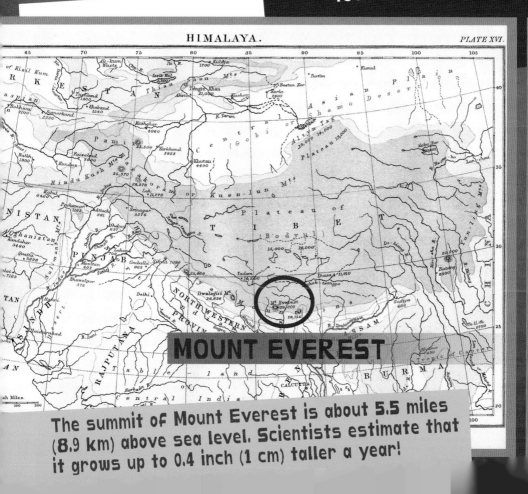

HIMALAYA.   PLATE XVI.

MOUNT EVEREST

The summit of Mount Everest is about **5.5** miles (**8.9** km) above sea level. Scientists estimate that it grows up to 0.4 inch (1 cm) taller a year!

SIR EVEREST

Mount Everest is named after Sir George Everest, who was the British surveyor general of India from 1830 to 1843. His job was to survey, or measure, different landforms and the distances between them so that maps could be made for future travelers. When he stopped working in 1843, Andrew Scott Waugh took his place to continue the project.

During their survey, Waugh and his team came across the mountain we now know as Mount Everest. At the time, the mountain was known as "Peak XV." The team preferred to use the local names for landforms, but Waugh and his team weren't aware of another name for Peak XV. He suggested it be named Mount Everest to honor Sir Everest. The name was officially approved in 1865.

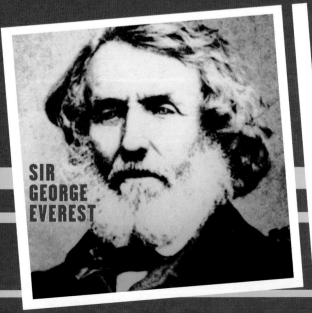

SIR GEORGE EVEREST

READING THE ROCKS

A THEODOLITE IS A TOOL THAT SURVEYORS USE TO VIEW PLACES IN THE DISTANCE AND MEASURE THE ANGLES BETWEEN THEM. WHEN WAUGH AND SIR EVEREST WERE COMPLETING THEIR SURVEYS IN THE MID-1800s, THEODOLITES WEIGHED OVER 1,000 POUNDS (453.6 KG)!

DIFFERENT NAMES

Although Waugh and his team didn't know it, there were local names for Mount Everest in Tibet and Nepal. In Tibet, the mountain was known as Chomolungma, which means "Goddess Mother of Mountains." In Nepal, people call it Sagarmatha, which means "Peak of Heaven." The rest of the world, however, now refers to it as Mount Everest.

It's unknown if Sir Everest ever saw Mount Everest in person. Some sources say it would have been unlikely, since he retired before the survey team went to Nepal.

7

MOVING CONTINENTS

How did something as **majestic** as Mount Everest form? Looking at a map could give you a clue. You may notice that some continents look like they could fit together like a puzzle. That may have been what Earth looked like 200 million years ago. It looked very different than it does today.

Scientists believe that almost all Earth's continents were once connected as a supercontinent called Pangaea. This name comes from a Greek word that means "all the Earth."

The answer to why the continents eventually moved apart can be found under Earth's surface. Earth is made of different layers that go miles deep under the ground. Geological processes that happen in these layers explain how the continents became separated millions of years ago.

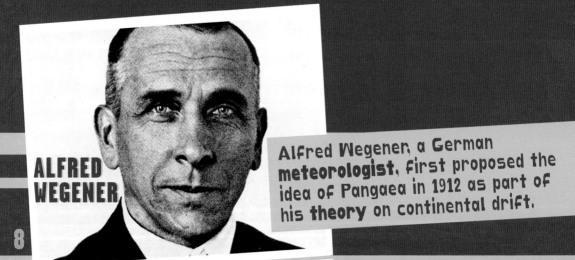

ALFRED WEGENER

Alfred Wegener, a German **meteorologist**, first proposed the idea of Pangaea in 1912 as part of his **theory** on continental drift.

1 PANGAEA

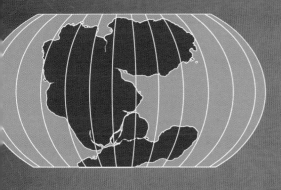

2

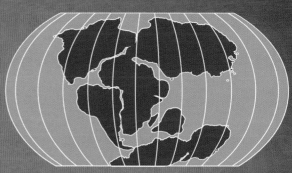

3

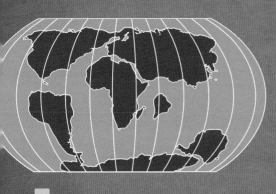

4 EARTH'S CONTINENTS TODAY

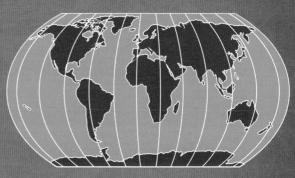

READING THE ROCKS

ALFRED WEGENER'S THEORY OF CONTINENTAL DRIFT DIDN'T EXPLAIN HOW THE CONTINENTS MOVED, ONLY THAT THEY DID. A CURRENT THEORY, CALLED PLATE TECTONICS, EXPLAINS THE PROCESSES THAT MADE PANGAEA BREAK APART OVER TIME.

BENEATH THE MOUNTAINS

The theory of plate tectonics explains how continents have moved over time, making Pangaea geological history. Earth's lithosphere is the crust and the upper part of the mantle, or the layer beneath the crust. According to this theory, the lithosphere is made of large pieces called tectonic plates. These plates sit on top of the lower part of the mantle. The rock here is soft, which allows the plates to float and glide over it.

Scientists believe Earth's plates started to move and break apart about 180 million years ago. About 55 million years ago, the Indian plate and Eurasian plate collided. The Eurasian plate is much bigger than the Indian plate, so the Indian plate was slowly pushed underneath it. The extreme pressure caused Earth's crust to rise. This is what caused the Himalayas and Mount Everest to form.

READING THE ROCKS

THE TECTONIC PLATES THAT FORMED THE HIMALAYAS MILLIONS OF YEARS AGO ARE STILL MOVING. TODAY, THESE PLATES MOVE 1 TO 2 INCHES (2.5 TO 5 CM) ANNUALLY. THIS MEANS THAT MOUNT EVEREST GETS A LITTLE TALLER EVERY YEAR.

UNDER THE SURFACE

The plate movement that causes Mount Everest to keep growing also creates a lot of **stress** within Earth's crust. After a while, the force of the two plates moving against each other causes the rocks on the edges to break, releasing pressure. When this high amount of pressure is released, it can cause earthquakes in the areas surrounding it.

There are many tectonic plates that make up Earth's surface. The seven largest are considered the main, or major, plates. The two plates that caused Mount Everest to form, the Eurasian plate and Indian plate, are major plates.

STUDYING EARTH

Geology is the study of Earth's history and its features. It includes the study of the matter that makes up our planet and different forces that change it. By studying geology, we can learn more about how our planet formed and how it changed over time. This, in turn, helps us understand the world around us today.

Geologists are people who spend their lives studying Earth's past, present, and future. They study major processes such as earthquakes, volcanic eruptions, and floods to determine why they happen and how they affect Earth's landscapes.

Some geologists research different matter on Earth, including water, metals, and rocks. Studying how different rocks form and change can help us learn more about Earth's history.

Some geologists study fossils, or records of life-forms that lived long ago. Fossils found on Mount Everest can tell us what conditions were like when these life-forms were alive.

HISTORY THROUGH ROCKS

Studying rocks tells us what life on Earth was like before we were here to study it. The different kinds of rocks found on Mount Everest can tell us about the different forces that shaped it.

Metamorphic rocks are made of other rocks whose properties changed over time. This happens when there's very high heat or pressure, which is comon in areas where tectonic plates meet. Igneous rocks are created when **magma** from deep inside Earth exits it, then cools as **lava** on its surface. When tectonic plates drift apart, there's a gap between them. The magma comes up through these gaps and the lava hardens, creating igneous rocks. Sedimentary rocks are also found on Mount Everest. They tell us even more about how it formed.

Because there's a lot of snow and ice covering Mount Everest, it can be difficult to see its different rock types.

LEARNING ABOUT THE PAST

Sedimentary rocks are created when wind and water break existing rocks down into smaller pieces called sediment. Over time, sediment may be carried by water or wind and deposited elsewhere. New sediments bury older sediments. Pressure squeezezs the older layers of sediment and eventually they become layers of rock. Limestone is one type of sedimentary rock found on the peak of Mount Everest.

People have found many fossils in the limestone of Mount Everest—including fossils from the sea! Millions of years ago, before the Indian and Eurasian plates collided, there was a sea between them called the Tethys Sea. After a long period of time, the plates collided with so much power that the Himalayas started to form under the sea. This pushed the ocean floor up to create the peaks we now know as the Himalaya mountain range.

Fossils of sea creatures that are millions of years old can be found in the Himalayas. The fossil pictured here is estimated to be roughly 65 million years old.

LOCATION OF ANCIENT TETHYS SEA

CHANGES WE CAN SEE

The theory of plate tectonics explains how Mount Everest formed over 50 million years ago, but other forces have changed it over time, too. Some are at work even today. These processes are called weathering and erosion.

Weathering is when natural forces break down rocks or minerals on the surface of Earth. Wind, water, and ice are forces of weathering that are constantly changing how Mount Everest looks. After the rocks are broken down, the process of erosion transports them, or moves them to another place. The sediment may be carried away by rain, melting ice and snow, or other means.

While the tectonic plates that originally formed Mount Everest are still moving closer together and adding height to the mountain, other forces such as weathering and erosion are wearing the mountain down at the same time.

READING THE ROCKS

THE APPALACHIAN MOUNTAINS IN NORTH AMERICA ONCE MAY HAVE BEEN TALLER THAN MOUNT EVEREST. THESE MOUNTAINS ARE OLDER THAN THE HIMALAYAS BY ABOUT 260 TO 460 MILLION YEARS. OVER TIME, FORCES SUCH AS WEATHERING AND EROSION HAVE WORN THEM DOWN.

A mass of ice causes erosion when it moves down the slope of a mountain. It can pick up and carry anything in its path.

CLIMATE CHANGE

Climate change is a big factor in the weathering and erosion we see on Mount Everest today. Since the 1990s, research has shown that the average temperature around Mount Everest has gone up by a few degrees. This temperature increase causes ice and snow to melt, which increases risks for climbers on Mount Everest. Research has shown that the amount of snowfall has been declining recently, too.

When snow falls but doesn't melt completely, time and pressure can turn it into masses of ice called glaciers. Higher temperatures cause the glaciers in the Himalayas and other areas on Earth to move and shrink. This can mean more dangerous **avalanches** for climbers, since higher temperatures can make chunks of ice break off and fall down the mountain faster.

The highest glacier in the world is the Khumbu Glacier on Mount Everest. One section of this glacier, the Khumbu Icefall, is one of the most dangerous climbing places in the world.

TO THE TOP

A successful journey to the top of Mount Everest and back takes a lot of training and preparation. People complete physical training for months or even years before their trip to prepare for the risks and problems they're almost certain to face. Climbers also need to research the routes and practice using their climbing equipment in advance.

An average **expedition** to the summit of Mount Everest takes about two months. Climbers encounter a lot of challenges on the way. Besides the cold temperatures and wind, it's very hard to breathe at such high **altitudes**. Almost all climbers bring along oxygen tanks to survive. The low oxygen levels can cause problems such as dizziness, headaches, and shortness of breath.

READING THE ROCKS

PEOPLE LEAVE A LOT OF TRASH ON MOUNT EVEREST. CLIMBERS LEAVE BEHIND FOOD CANS, EMPTY OXYGEN BOTTLES, DAMAGED CAMPING EQUIPMENT, AND OTHER ITEMS. THE GOVERNMENT AND LOCALS TRY TO KEEP THE AREA CLEAN, BUT IT REMAINS A BIG PROBLEM.

A DEADLY JOURNEY

More than 4,000 people have tried to climb Mount Everest, but not all survive the journey. When someone dies on Mount Everest, their body is usually left on the mountain because weather conditions and low oxygen levels make it so difficult to remove. Over time, the locations of certain bodies left on the mountain have come to serve as landmarks for parts of the route.

Sherpas are the local people who serve as guides and experts for climbing the mountain. Many climbers depend on Sherpas to get to their destination, or end point, safely.

A SAFER JOURNEY

New **technology** has helped climbers make the journey to climb Mount Everest more safely than they could before. When early climbers were making the journey, they didn't have the advanced equipment and gear that's available to us now.

The suits that climbers wear today are more breathable and waterproof than they were in the past. Tents are more lightweight, and they can handle the very cold temperatures and wind much better. Oxygen tanks are now much lighter to carry.

These advances have improved the safety and health of climbers, but there are some things we can't solve. The rocky landscape and size of Mount Everest can make it very hard or very dangerous to climb. There are many **remote** places that can't be accessed at all.

A GLIMPSE INTO THE PAST

When the bodies of climbers who died on Mount Everest are found decades later, the equipment they used on their journey is often found with them. This can give us a glimpse into what kinds of equipment they used and how much it has changed from what climbers use today.

The two Everest base camps are where climbers camp out before they make their way up or down the mountain. For some people, their goal is to reach one of the base camps rather than the summit because that's more achievable.

ADVANCES IN TECHNOLOGY

How do scientists study Mount Everest when the journey there can be so dangerous and sometimes even deadly? Advances in technology help us study the mountain and its patterns.

Satellites can be used to learn more about Mount Everest. Images from satellites help us create maps of the mountain and show us how it changes over time.

Another example is the time-lapse camera that was set up at the Khumbu Icefall. The camera takes a photo every 30 minutes. Over time, these photos are used to see how much the glacier is melting and when certain pieces of ice might fall. Using this **data**, scientists can estimate when the area will be safest to cross.

This is an image taken of Mount Everest from a satellite. Satellites give us the chance to see Earth's landforms from space.

USING THE PAST TO PREDICT THE FUTURE

We've learned how Mount Everest formed by studying rocks, fossils, and Earth's processes. We can also measure its changes every year and then use this information to predict how it will look in the future.

Scientists think the glaciers on Mount Everest will continue to melt due to climate change. Some studies have shown that certain glaciers could even disappear completely by the year 2100. This could cause flooding and prevent towns in the area from getting fresh water.

Since tectonic plates are always moving, so is Mount Everest. It moves about 1.5 inches (4 cm) northeast each year. Scientists can use this data to predict how the movement will change the Himalayas and how it could affect Nepal and Tibet in the future.

Other natural forces besides plate tectonics and weathering affect Mount Everest. A very destructive earthquake in Nepal in 2015 is said to have moved Mount Everest by 1.18 inches (3 cm).

READING THE ROCKS

The world around us is always changing. Sometimes we can see the changes, but others happen much more slowly and over millions of years.

We've learned a lot about how Mount Everest formed, but there's still a lot more out there for us to discover. Studying rocks gives us the chance to see what life on Earth was like millions of years ago. Changes in technology have helped us learn how Mount Everest was created and how different forces such as rising temperatures and weathering continue to change it today.

By studying geology, we can learn how our planet has changed over time and what we can expect to happen to it in the future.

GLOSSARY

altitude: The height of something above the sea.

avalanche: A mass of snow, ice, and rocks rapidly falling down a mountainside.

climate change: Change in Earth's weather caused by human activity.

data: Information, often presented as numbers.

expedition: A journey undertaken by a group of people for a particular purpose.

lava: Hot, liquid, or soft rock located above the surface of Earth.

magma: Hot, liquid, or soft rock located below the surface of Earth.

majestic: Awe-inspiring.

meteorologist: Someone who studies the weather.

remote: Far away.

satellite: A machine that travels around the earth or moon or another planet in order to collect information about it.

stress: Pressure applied to an object.

summit: The highest point of a mountain.

technology: The use of knowledge to invent new tools.

theory: An idea or principle that explains facts or events.

INDEX

WEBSITES

Due to the changing nature of Internet links, PowerKids Press has developed an online list of websites related to the subject of this book. This site is updated regularly. Please use this link to access the list: www.powerkidslinks.com/EHTR/everest